Whatever you desire

Some an army of horsemen, some an army on foot
and some say a fleet of ships is the loveliest sight
on this dark earth; but I say it is whatever you desire

       Sappho
       translated by Josephine Balmer

Poems copyright © The authors 1990
This selection copyright © The Oscars Press 1990
Introduction copyright © Mary Jo Bang 1990
Reprinted 1991
ISBN 0 9512581 9 2

The Oscars Press, BM Oscars, London WC1N 3XX

All rights reserved. No part of this publication may be reproduced, stored in a retrieval system, or transmitted, in any form or by any means, electronic, mechanical, photocopying, recording or otherwise, without prior permission.

Cover photograph: Chateau de Chambord, France, by Mary Jo Bang

Cover design by Pictures Pens Lens, 42 Pitman House, Tanners Hill, London SE8 4PT

Typesetting by Counter Productions, PO Box 556, London SE5 0RL

Printed and bound by Billing & Sons, Worcester

The Oscars Press is a member of the Association of Little Presses, and the Small Press Group.

Financially assisted by Greater London Arts

Also published by the Oscars Press:

Paperback:
Take Any Train: a book of gay men's poetry edited by Peter Daniels

Pamphlets include:
Teatime at Sarah's: poems by Dee Shelley, Beryl Colquhoun, Sarah Walker, Kathryn Bell, Ger Killeen, and a short story by Elsa Beckett
Sugar & Snails: an Oscars mixture

WHATEVER YOU DESIRE

A Book of Lesbian Poetry

Edited by Mary Jo Bang

The Oscars Press

ACKNOWLEDGEMENTS

There are many people who make hidden but significant contributions in a book such as this. Peggy Shinner was particularly helpful and very generously spent much time helping me think through what made these poems special for me. For that, and for years of friendship, I thank her. Thanks, also, to Ann Tyler for advice and encouragement and to all of the poets involved in the Oscars for extending me the privilege of editing this collection. Finally, I would like to thank the women who sent their work. Of the choices I made, I can only say that they reflect my own biases, both of style and content. In the end, I hope they strike a responsive cord in those who read them.

The following have appeared elsewhere:

Sappho, *Poems and Fragments* translated by Josephine Balmer, Brilliance Books, 1984.

Aspen, "Loving Song", in *Spinster*, No.3

Astra, "funeral in new york", "pussy willow", and "spirit" from *Back You Come, Mother Dear*, Virago, 1986.

Mary Jo Bang, "In A Book Of Original Entry" in *Earth's Daughters* (USA) No.35, and "Open Heart Surgery" in *Poetry Nottingham* Vol.43 No.3.

Jennifer Barraclough, "The Watch Cottage", in *The North*, 1987.

Kathryn Bell, "Nothing Like This Before" in *Sugar & Snails*, Oscars Press, 1990.

Mandy Dee (Caroline Halliday, literary executrix), "Night", in *Sinister Wisdom* (USA).

Maureen Duffy, "On the London Poetry Secretariat Poet's Card", "Genetics", and "Preserves", from *Collected Poems*, Hamish Hamilton, 1985.

U.A.Fanthorpe, "You Will Be Hearing From Us Shortly" and "On Buying OS Sheet 163" from *Standing To*, Peterloo Poets, 1982, and "Horticultural Show" from *Side Effects*, Peterloo Poets, 1978.

Caroline Griffin, "Making Something For My Mother", "If My Life Could Be Simple", and "Elizabeth", from *Passion is Everywhere Appropriate*, Onlywomen Press, 1989.

Ger Killeen, "To Her Lover", in *Sugar & Snails*, Oscars Press, 1990.

Dorothy Nimmo, "Coming Out" and "Dorsets Lambing", from *Homewards*, Giant Steps Press, 1987.

Sarah Walker, "Discreet" and "Poem", in *Teatime at Sarah's*, Oscars Press, 1989.

CONTENTS

Introduction   7

Eleanor Dare   9
   One Hundred Moments
   UFO

Dorothy Nimmo   11
   Coming Out
   Dorsets Lambing
   The Tangles of Neaera's Hair

Jeannie Brehaut   14
   daughter in outer space
   everything i said last night was true
   letter to a friend

Caroline Griffin   18
   Making Something for my Mother
   If my life could be simple
   Elizabeth

Suzanna Rasmussen   23
   Constancy

Caroline Halliday   25
   demons
   Through air

Mandy Dee   30
   Night

Sarah Walker   32
   Poem
   Indiscreet

U.A. Fanthorpe   35
   You will be hearing from us shortly
   On Buying OS Sheet 163
   Horticultural Show

Annie Blue   39
   What colour shall I name you?
   UB40 Queue Blues
   Postcard

Kathleen O'Donnell   42
   Storytime

Jennifer Barraclough   44
   The Watch Cottage

Kathryn Bell   45
   Nothing Like This Before

Shirani Situnayake   46
   SOMETIMES I THINK THERE IS A CONSPIRACY
   I USED TO SEEK THE REGULAR FAMILIAR

Ann Slade 48
  To Jane
Jan Sellers 49
  Where Lesbians Come From
Margaret Easton 50
  On Ironing
  Across the Sand
Astra 52
  funeral in new york
  pussy willows
  spirit
Maureen Duffy 55
  On the London Poetry Secretariat's Poet's Card
  Genetics
  Preserves
Berta Freistadt 58
  Reprimand
Shirley Picton 60
  we can't think every issue through
  memories
Ger Killeen 62
  To Her Lover
Louise Carolin 63
  here we are again
  in a world where words
Maggie Christie 65
  Listening to the radio 2nd of february 1988
  cottaging
Mary Jo Bang 66
  In A Book of Original Entry
  I Am Writing
  Open Heart Surgery
Gillian Hanscombe 70
  From "Some of Sybil":
  In the guise
  Does she know
Aspen 71
  loving song
Kate Hall 72
  Eye Catching
Gillian Spraggs 74
  Riddle Game
Kyde Willowmoon 75
  One Minute
Biographical notes 77

INTRODUCTION

Whatever You Desire is a collection of lesbian poetry by British and expatriate women living in Britain. The poems speak of our many desires in all their modern manifestations. They describe the journeys on which we have set sail to make of our lives richly textured experiences. They give voice to the sacrifices we sometimes must make, our defeats and victories, our frustrations and celebrations.

Our passions are not singularly sexual (Jan Sellers' witty poem, "Where Lesbians Come From", notwithstanding). As often we write about reaching out as sisters and friends, mothers and daughters. In writing, we try to distill our experiences into those few sharp words which can cut through the walls which divide us. We know what we are up against. The challenge which each of us faces is summed up in the first lines of Eleanor Dare's poem "One Hundred Moments":

> *The whole of a life has to go into this poem: the frou-frou of my mother's summer dresses under her beetle-black Singer two months after I was born. The fathomless tedium of London suburbs in the 1960's.*

One of our most ardent longings is for reconciliation with the past. We strive for an uneasy peace with those amorphous spirits which seem never to settle. In Astra's poem, "spirit", she writes about the ubiquitous presence of the deceased mother:

> next year i'll plant lilacs
> in my garden
> one white one purple
>
> then i'll know she's really with me
> as i know she's in the pussy willows
> i've cut from my garden
> and keep in a tall pottery jug
> in front of my window
> that looks out onto the woods
>
> she's out there too

Yet, as Jennifer Barraclough writes in "The Watch Cottage", *This is no ghost reviving exercise.* While we may begin in the past, we hope the road will lead us somewhere new.

We would, if only we could, face death squarely. Caroline Halliday's poignant poem, "Through Air", written for Mandy Dee, reminds us of the limits of our understanding. It is as if only the dying can truly separate the aesthetic from the reality of death. Mandy Dee writes in "Night":

> *Suddenly no more stars tonight*
> *Sickness creeps along my spine*
> *I return to the mundane*
> *abandoning philosophy*
> *for warmth and paracetamol*
> *breath out*
> *breath out*
> *breath out*

For all of this, we are not mired in introspection or retrospection. We live in the real world; we are expert witnesses to living. We explore our sexuality, our own anger, mother our children, and — as Suzanna Rasmussen says in "Constancy" — *dream of / more than / more than.*

It is the political world which U.A. Fanthorpe details with chilling irony in "You Will Be Hearing From Us Shortly". It is the painful world of Dorothy Nimmo's "Dorsets Lambing", where the poet looks on while a neighbor helps a ewe with a difficult delivery. Afterwards:

> *carry the two, legs dangling, to the pen*
> *making lamb noises so the ewe will follow*
> *trailing her blood and slime. Her flanks*
> *look empty now. All night she suffers*
> *her ruptured womb and in the morning dies.*
> *Years of experience, he knew what to do*
> *and I knew nothing. Except how it feels.*

All of the poets in this book write about "how it feels". In doing so, they add their testimony to a growing literary tradition, a tradition which speaks with honesty and eloquence of our deepest desires.

Mary Jo Bang

ELEANOR DARE

One Hundred Moments

I

The whole of a life has to go in this poem: the frou-frou of my mother's summer dresses under her beetle black Singer — two months after I was born. A premature bantling. Nagging at her boredom threshold. The fathomless tedium of London suburbs in the 1960's. Turgid beyond idiocy. Driving my mother into sudden escape. My father — trillionaire of husbandly grief, hidden in his work. His four children beguiled by moon travel, motherships. Micro tea sets, shrivelled museum heads.

II

Five years of fearing child assassins. Murderers around every corner in this child hating city. Swimming instructors who touched our baby breasts. The drab terrain of schooldays. The rickety click of my final train ride away from home. Thinking lovers would cartwheel down the aisles towards me — couriers of free play and rowdiness.

III

Then in this Megalopolis, the drabbest houses were voluptuous. And even by the disgraceful Thames an old ship's figurehead winked at me. A vulgar and intimate signal. I stroked her breasts — realising I was mad and Lesbian. Suddenly encircled by dangerous punk Dykes — furious and base born. They were kind to me. Thievish smash and grab girls who stole me sensual merchandize: warm clothes. Strong boots with yellow stitching. Their baroque ritual love making benevolent and exhilarated. Helicopters of the river, buzzing above our heads. Gray Thames fug filling our lungs.

IV

The whole of a life accelerated into euphoric momentum. The trains chattering an end to tedium. The finishing stroke of dead pan listlessness. Cranes at the dock dropping their burden of corporate malice. My foul spoken friends dancing on the old factory roof, singing: "Threaten, Swear, Take revenge, Speak evil, Devitalize your enemies, Press overdrive, Denounce Consortiums, and above all — Dissent."

UFO

This was the time of
Flying Saucer cults,
of girls circling round school playgrounds with
tartan scarves —
Bay City Roller girls
dancing and spinning their fearful girl
fever. Excluding boys, and embryo Lesbians
like me.
Who hated French elastic and fancied neither Starsky nor
Hutch.
Arrogantly disdaining her friend's Cindy doll
and her full range of
fabulous accessories.

I wanted to
swim the Channel before I was twelve,
explore the Arctic circle,
invent a machine for resurrecting dinosaurs
and finally find a
Flying Saucer club that didn't think I
was too young
to share the
secrets of
the universe.

DOROTHY NIMMO

Coming Out

There is a door. Believe me. Open it.
You are inside of your own volition.
Can you see the light under the lintel?
Run your hand along the door jamb.
What makes you think you are locked in?
You have no reason. I am trying to help you.

If you shut your eyes you may feel better.
There must be a handle of some sort.
Now when your fingers fumble
over the latch, sneck, knob, spindle
see if it turns. Perhaps if you pull
sharply you'll find it gives.
Try moving to the right. There is
almost certainly some special trick
you have to learn. Manipulate.
Juggle. Shift. Do not lose your head.
Trust me. When the door opens
you will see the assembled faces.

And by their expression you can imagine
what you have become.

Dorsets Lambing

First year; the first lot of ewes brought in
favour their sore feet in the straw
and move their jaws on silage. There's one
her flanks spread wide panting a little.
Corner her. Between drapes of daggled wool
her flesh is pink and swollen, secretive.
Now find the opening, plunge the hand in, so.
She's tight. Her passage clamps my wrist.
Warm slime round bone lumps in a bone cage.
Pull now. Pull gently. A shift towards me:
I shut my eyes and slurp
out on the straw a long wet lamb smeared yellow.
Clear mouth of mucus, slap the ribs again.
It's breathing, bleats. Heave it up front
she'll clean it now and there's another coming.

Blunt muzzle, blind eyes, one hoof only.
The tongue's stuck out. There's something wrong.
No time to lose, go round for Jack next door.
(years of experience, he'll know what to do).
Briskly he grabs the head and shoves it back.
Squatting across her neck I feel her strain.
Buried to the elbow in her prison body
he rummages, slops. Leg's back, he says,
I'll have to turn it. Let go girl.
I can smell lanolin, sheep shit, afterbirth.
Seems a long time. Push mother. Something gives.
It's all right now, it's done. He leans
to blow in the slack mouth slip slop the sides
Fine little tups, look at the size! You're lucky
She'll be off colour for a day or so.
Good thing you called me. Any time, he says.

Carry the two, legs dangling, to the pen
making lamb noises so the ewe will follow
trailing her blood and slime. Her flanks
look empty now. All night she suffers
her ruptured womb and in the morning dies.
Years of experience, he knew what to do
and I knew nothing. Except how it feels.

The Tangles of Neaera's Hair

Neaera
in her flaming hair
clasps salamanders
triple-tongued; only
strong spirits face them out.

Combs down pale shoulders
amber waterfalls, or
on an ebbing tide
emptying the rockpool, bronze
tendrils waver
set with pearls.

Pins her lovelocks high
cloud cover parting
a blue streak; up there
beyond the cirrus
sickle swifts
continually play.

Plaits her hair with serpents,
weaves in those dreadlocks all
their lost entangled faces

(keep your eyes closed
climbing up
your fingers crossed).

Wild girl, her hair
a mess of cirrus,
seaweed,
flame.

JEANNIE BREHAUT

daughter in outer space

child of mine light up this city tonight
i'm calling you home
my first   only ever born
brave woman rider.

it was you invented the night

sailed the moon out of the sky
left my house   floating
in darkness, who you say
is your friend, your cover.
afterwards
all that was left of you
one silver moon in every cupboard
letters from girls
on other planets
you could make love to

your skin will turn green if you keep up that.

i've cried a river to bring you home
this planet has turned four times since you left me.
you must have star-crossed
my hard feelings
i look for you anew
in all the old places
we used to
moonwatch.

my plan:
to change the course of our small history
charge this house up every night like a space station.
if it's not too late
land here   please
i need you.

i am your earth mother.
i know how you happened.

everything i said last night was true

everything i said last night was true
i have never before
& you were
my hands don't want to be leaving
my feet are having trouble
finding the door
as well   you know

i'm still that person
i'll never forget your
non-stop kissing
know-it-all fingers
the secret way you fold your clothes just so
before you come to bed
then tie my ankles
& wrists
with silk
without asking
the happy surprise that anybody
anymore
would do that
the middle of the night with you is
something else
i love your face when you tease me
the way you laugh
say   look no hands
move fast as   you
slow & deep
all night
watch me
come morning i'm sore and you're grumpy
making love hard is
our only thing
we get

i have to go because i do
everything we are together is just so

never before
& crazy

go far enough in me & i will beat for you
call your real name
almost make us both
more   happy
before we stop
stand up
start fighting about something stupid
i hate that

this is not a way back home
i can't take being hurt
& wanting it from you
cruelty is complicated as
anything
after a while
you'll think you dreamed me
hands safe in my pockets
you touch me too hard
like nobody
i'm leaving

the things you have to do
every minute
make their own sense

letter to a friend

i'm in love   sarah   there's this girl
at war with her chosen power
no room in any of her stories
everything is wrong.

she doesn't believe
i would wait for her
i don't know what she has coming
she's a girl
not a woman
child she may never uncover
we were & now we're not
potent enough for this time.

she & i both escaped
from the same blame childhood
i should have met her then   sarah
travelling thru'
forward & back
in love with a hot girl
losing power.

       i am afraid of
being in pieces
what i don't remember
how broken i once was
we still are.

CAROLINE GRIFFIN

Making Something for my Mother

Find driftwood from the garden —
brown damp not salt
I light a candle. The wood is
broken off and the grain exposed
ridges   the grain of a wave.

The last time I saw my mother
she held my hand as we walked
down the narrow and precarious steps
of a hotel. Her hand was hot.
I think she was nervous.

And what did I say? Nothing.
We hugged in the Ladies Powder Room.
I think we did. Toiled back upstairs.
There were small cakes and a man
at a piano played Chopin —
not as well as my mother.

Her hands were hot and nervous.
I melt wax   tear small pieces of tissue.
I want flakes of gold to anoint her.
The wind howls between corridors
of Himalayan mountains and in the
gasping pain of high altitude
another stone is rolled to the cairn.

Though dead you are still my mother.
Her flag flies above them all
trailing a cry in thin cold air.
May grief not whip a garland to shreds.
The wind can spin out streamers
perfumed with her name   a fine thread

that will go down any valley
we choose to remember or forget —
the spun name encircling Tibetan stones
polished by rain from higher mountains.
On the roof of the world
her name is a blazon.

She powdered her face.
We toiled back upstairs. Now is
wood and clay   paper and candle-light
to melt and burn   score and flame over.
No trumpet can sound her name loud enough.

I write her name in pencil
on tissue-paper. Against a twig
upright in the wood a fragment
of wax secures it   translucent and
I add more flags   prayer-flags,
to what is now a tree   a mast.

If my life could be simple

If my life could be simple
a brush stroke on a page
you would be there.
And in this shape I make with my hands
you would see a life moving.

river   I want you to touch me
mountain   we hold this space between us
fiercely   mountain   we push against
our hands, our bodies   hold the choice, the space —
ocean   you move on top of me   ocean
your mouth   your tongue presses
choosing again and again   river
I want you to touch me.

Each touch says

              this is how our lives have been
              and this is how we could be.
Each touch makes a life
            more vivid and more possible.
"We are more than we know."
"There is no such thing as coincidence."

I bend to kiss your neck   tender says the kiss
tenderness   your powerful shoulders move
reaching towards my breast   you place
my nipple in your mouth   around you
there is all that I can be of mother
here at the edge of you
holding   respectful.
You can call this love or work.

Our bodies move   our hands touch.
We are more than we know
and meaning rises to meet this touching
creates a new land to walk on
solid surprise at the bend of a river.

I speak of land   but this is creation
how we become more. Our passion breathes
the child in us, not just the past accepted
but the life in us   as vital as
        the kicking baby
            in the amniotic sac —
how can we touch without
        a raging to create
        more space, more life
or knowing that
        tomorrow I can go back
        and trace my footprints?

I want to use all this
gather it up with energy
like a traveller beginning —
knowing the many shrines I've made
to silence fear with beauty.

The passion in my stride contains this fear.
This ground-swell breathing
is what I have despised   it is myself.

I want now to straddle the lashed boards
straining on the waves.
This is not the best I can do
the best is a line of effort
the edge of the waves where the rubble collects —
This is how I move
with you   with myself   to
remember   learn and invent.

Elizabeth

Elizabeth — this formality
marks the difference between now and then,
Lizzie — I want to say
we convent schoolgirls were heroic lovers,
unsupported explorers.
What we did put us outside the world we knew
and for a time we held together.

I wanted your certainty
kneeling with you in the church by the river
then watching the floods.
A precise vision I had
the boat slicing through water
wanting to see how it curled how it
washed the bank
and spread   over the pathways.

Remember the world we stepped out of —
the porcelain madonnas   the virtues of silence
men in suits   flickering electric signs —
the boy I kissed on the river-bank
his hand cupping my breast
his leg taut and nervous against mine.
Boys did this and   I gave you a warning
trying to say what the world had taught me.

You climb into bed with me
it is impossible to believe   we touch each other
turning away from the world inside me
not that
we were tender   engrossed   but straitened
so straitened   by silence
the narrow bed   your sleeping sister.
We suffered a passion of reaching out
so cramped we bruised each other.
And in the morning the shock of how we felt
the bruises on our breasts —
we needed wider times.

Remember what they did to us?
Those who were masked —
The teacher walking by who watched us kissing.
The nun whose mask slipped
gripping the table   rising with anger
she asked you what we did —
and searched my poems to find out.
The others used no words.
They did not speak, just sideways sarcasm
and fear. Your phone-call jerked my father's mocking
"Don't forget to say you love her."

Did they know more than we did?

Going on for a year
no one took care of us
there were no celebrations.
We were lovers, climbers
held by nothing but our feelings.
We searched for clarity and comfort
and they shook us, shook us badly.

A rope still trails between us
reach out   grasp it   angry —
see what we had and what was taken from us?
Refuse to let it go.

SUZANNA RASMUSSEN

Constancy

The den of when
was
held
by
the number two

The hive of lust
was
felled
by
the thunder of three

The thought of worst
was
cursed
by
a teller of nought

Constancy was forever
growing on my left
shoulder until a
mole called forlorn
crawled through
my nasal passages
& spat out God
& at last I knew
I was forever a
mere clod of
earth in the
mildest hemisphere
called loving
& loved & moving
& till then —

Yes my hair
was just
a bit of
fuck
in the
air
my toes
were
squew whiff
I felt a hint
of your contempt
& suddenly
I dreamed of
more than
more than.

CAROLINE HALLIDAY

demons

eyeball/
naked
neurotic/
demons

        the body is a tulip
        labia
        petals
        a dirt track
        why are these things
        so close

        an iris folded
        I plunge my hand
        sudden
        feeling my own knot
        arsehole cervix from
        the inside
        the body soft
        ageing

past hopefulness

        a shape open
        bones in the sky

        ladder

pinnioned
between joy and death   decay
bones strung between me and flesh
flesh over fingers   bones
I want to push to the limits now

I want to push to the limits now

one: the body yelps
              creases wrinkles
              irregularities
     (push to the limits)
              the sweat the sheen on it
              it lives glory
              temporary
              (in 500 years
              nothing)
              it is now with the sheen on it
              my sheened flesh

              the body yelps
              there are flocks   teeming thousands
              sensation explodes   (numbed dulled)
              this is just mine
              (and I cannot reach it)
              vulnerable perishable
              a house of caves
                      stacked
              that I ignore

push to the limits
(two) : the work to write this down

There are spaces between me and others
              I'm afraid of
              push away away
              that I'm afraid of   *: (three)*

You promise responses   *: (four)*
              freedom is a touch answered in kind
              you are a knot I push against   solid
              responsive

demons;   *this is not possible*
demons;   *there are too many people*
                      I owe them
                      nothing was single   nothing
                      guilt

pain in the head   built on top of pain
denials
clarity worn thin like a doormat
dusty falling apart

demons; why do these things change
                white frocks   sickness
                I wasn't
                        I wasn't
                I didn't mean to
                how should I know
                how
                should I know
                there was nothing explained

demons are dirt in the skin
                skin in the dirt
                frock in the dirt

five: this time   to eat   listen   walk   naked
                    freely   is so
                    limited

such a limit   refutation
                  of years

                              to know freedom
                              is unwise
                              (not like the others)

this hour between 3 and 6
alone

                I am angry
                FUCKING ANGRY
                you perverted
                my sense:
                          of freedom
                my sense:
                          of love
                my
                senses

push them
>> *to*
>> *the*
>> *limits*

push them to the limits
and fear the consequences
>> *I don't know how/to*
>> *choose*
>> *to take my time*
>> *to make decisions*
>> *to look you in the face*
>> *and say   I don't want to*
>> *or*

>> *I don't know*
>> *if*
>> *I want to*

to walk   lie   naked   dance
in this my house
between 3 and 6
in the afternoon
angry

twisting my neck through

>> *to die*
>> *die*
>> *unabsolved*

absolved of other people's
>> *demands   :don't*
>>> *:ever*

Through air

for Mandy Dee 3.8.52 - 30.10.88

If we could put a slice through time
and through the air,
like a picasso give life   two facets,
one would be for me, and one for you;
and down the joining line, life would venture in
and venture out.

If you go there, I thought, I'll follow.
I'd go with you, if it were possible
to go, and hold your hand,
and come back.

     Somewhere a flower opens
(only for itself? for us?)
in my palm the tiny ribs of the poppy head,
designed — created —
and that minute snail, its shell transparent,
its movement purposeful.
Someone designed this, I said, for fun.

If you go there, I'll follow.
One part of me there with you,
in the pit of my belly, in the saliva on my tongue,
and other parts run to hide
— *I don't know what it is to be alive* —

We held each other, in the dark room;
I told you all I have to tell about death —
the time I was back inside my seven-year-old life
— *you cannot go back   you are there now* —
and about Colleen,   choosing to explore what happens next.
I think of her there, sometimes,   ready to greet me,
when I slide through the joining line, the two facets of time.

Mandy, I want to share the journey —
(mitigate the fear
             if I could)
and stay on this raw edge of living;
reach out my hand into the air.

MANDY DEE

Night

All my senses are wrapped
In glass, pinched and dry

I look to my past
When I accepted fiercely
the crackle and flashes of light
then my spastic booted
feet crashed thro' the night-street.
So I created minute
earthly sparks to match heaven's stars
and I loved my small striding;
resounding my presence to others —
the quiet walkers
and bland straight standers.

Mostly now my itching creeping senses
comprehend only what my hands and feet can reach.
I lie as if asleep
day by half existent day
in this room
womb of growing multiple sclerosis
tomb of my old strength
life flickering in the darkness.

And I have found a severe delight
that without life death is
uncreated and undead
Death to be must first defer to life.

If the universe and mine utterly disintegrate
                    and unbecome
death must disperse into chaos
and the root of all creation cease.

So though restrained within one room
and my flashes of defiance
are now restless sclerotic jabs
and hardly painless;
I proclaim
death interspaced eternally
by life, then life

Suddenly no more stars tonight
Sickness creeps along my spine
I return to the mundane
abandoning philosophy
for warmth and paracetamol
breath out
breath out
breath out

                          16th October 1985

SARAH WALKER

Poem

This is a poem that I wrote the other day.

This is a poem that I've just written. I'm not quite sure about it yet but here it is anyway and I hope you like it.

This is a poem that kept me awake half the night, waiting for the contractions, holding on for the moment when the waters break and the birth begins.

This is a poem that was typed out in the top room of a house full of creaks and whispers, the neighbours must have thought I'd flipped.

This is a poem with a purpose, a poem with a message, a poem full of blood and rage and tenderness. I wrote it the other day, I hope you like it.

This is a poem scribbled on a fumbled sheet, penned on vellum, misprinted on a handout that got thrown away, sprayed in scarlet paint over by the dustbins.

This is a poem folded in half and half again, sealed in an envelope and posted to an address I have forgotten. This is a poem on rice paper to be memorised and eaten. This is a poem for people who can't read.

This is a poem with a meaning, a poem that says what it wants to say only with the wrong words and using the wrong voice.

This is a poem that disappears up its own fundamental inconsistencies.

This is a poem that drops from a clear sky onto a crowded street,
touching each upturned face like a thousand bits of paper
scattered from a passing plane.

This is for you to murmur to your lover, moving in your arms on a
sticky afternoon. This is a poem for you to wrap yourself in
against the cold, for you to write with your breath on the sky of
a starry night. This is a poem chanted on the streets before the
guns begin, this is for the smokey upper rooms of pubs, all it
needs is a backing track and a contract.

This is a poem that turns itself into food and water and health for a
hundred thousand million people and gets sent to the wrong
country, the wrong continent, the wrong planet, the one where
the famine isn't.

This is a poem you will forget tomorrow, or in half an hour, laughed
off with the next joke, downed with the next pint, left on the
motorway at the mercy of the wheels.

This is a poem that got halfway there, that seemed like a good idea
when it started, before I read it, before I wrote it, before I let it
down and it let me.

This is a poem that I wrote the other day, I'm not quite sure about it
yet but there it is anyway, thanks, I hope you like it, thanks.

Indiscreet

Multi-coloured we were not discreet
but gorgeous as parrots in a green tree,
kaleidoscopic marchers
in a confluence of tongues
and brilliance of banners.
Afterwards, after making love in the van
with the rain patting on the roof
I dreamt that we were making love in the van
while outside the marchers
parted around us in a flood of faces
lit up like a bed of flowers
in a rainy municipal park when suddenly the sun
places her feet upon the petals.

U. A. FANTHORPE

You will be hearing from us shortly

You feel adequate to the demands of this position?
What qualities do you feel you
Personally have to offer?

                                    Ah

Let us consider your application form.
Your qualifications, though impressive, are
Not, we must admit, precisely what
We had in mind. Would you care
To defend their relevance?

                                    Indeed

Now your age. Perhaps you feel able
To make your own comment about that,
Too? We are conscious ourselves
Of the need for a candidate with precisely
The right degree of immaturity.

                                  So glad we agree

And now a delicate matter: your looks.
You do appreciate this work involves
Contact with the actual public? Might they,
Perhaps, find your appearance
Disturbing?

                                  Quite so

And your accent. That is the way
You have always spoken, is it? What
Of your education? Were
You educated? We mean, of course,
Where were you educated?
                                          And how
Much of a handicap is that to you,
Would you say?

                    Married, children,
We see. The usual dubious
Desire to perpetuate what had better
Not have happened at all. We do not
Ask what domestic disasters shimmer
Behind that vaguely unsuitable address.

And you were born —?

                                                    Yes. Pity.

So glad we agree.

On Buying OS Sheet 163

I own all this. Not loutish acres
That tax the spirit, but the hawking
Eye's freehold, paper country.

Thirtytwo inches of aqueduct,
Windmill (disused), club house, embankment,
Public conveniences

In rural areas. This is my
landlocked landscape that lives in cipher,
And is truer than walking.

Red and imperial, the Romans
Stride eastward. Mysterious, yellow,
The Salt Way halts and is gone.

Here, bigger than the hamlets they are,
Wild wayside syllables stand blooming:
Filkins, Lechlade, Broughton Poggs.

Here only I discard the umber
Reticulations of sad cities,
The pull and drag of mud.

Horticultural Show

These are Persephone's fruits
Of the underyear. These will guide us
Through the slow dream of winter.

Onions her paleskinned lamps.
Rub them for strange knowledge. They shine
With the light of the tomb.

Drawn in fine runes along
hard green rinds, the incomprehensible
Initiation of the marrow.

All orange energy driven
Down to a final hair, these carrots
Have been at the heart of darkness.

And parti-coloured leeks,
Their green hair plaited, like Iroquois braves,
Leaning exhausted in corners.

Holystoned the presence
Of potatoes, pure white and stained pink.
Persephone's bread.

Sacrificed beetroots
Display their bleeding hearts. We read
The future in these entrails.

Out in the world excitable
Ponies caper, Punch batters Judy, a man
Creates a drystone wall in thirty minutes,

Arrows fly, coconuts fall, crocodiles
And Jubilee mugs, disguised as children,
Cope with candyfloss, the band
Adds its slow waltz heart beat.

Here in the tent, in the sepia hush,
Persephone's fruits utter where they have been,
Where we are going.

ANNIE BLUE

What colour shall I name you?

Turquoise or maybe magenta
or Maxfield Parrish blue
when you sing.
Making love you are
iridescent opal or
flashes of amber and ochre
with shocks of pure, raw crimson.
Sometimes I see
marcasite in the
turn of your head.
Jade for your voice
veiling shades of sepia.
Your smile is delightfully
apricot, laced with burgundy
but when I catch you
looking at me like that,
you are absolutely
deepest indigo,
shot through with
tiny threads of topaz.

UB40 Queue Blues

here come the UB40 queue blues
the dirty wall fuck it all
come to claim my due blues

here come the thursday a.m. grime time
the stand in line number nine
crazy pantomime time

here come the thirty minute hate show
you're not there deadly stare
i'm gonna make you wait show

here come the just another face race
scrounging mob aint got no job
so you'd better know your place race

here come the UB40 queue blues
the dirty wall fuck it all
come to claim my due blues

Postcard

I let go and
it will never stop,
never
never
never stop.
You never came,
never,
you sent me
a postcard.

Alone at the end,
tied in knots
as everything comes
crashing around,
pouring pain
down the phone
but you never came
never
never
never came,
you sent me
a postcard;

it said:–

"Dear Annie,
Mum and I are sitting in
a little Tea Garden in
East Bergholt musing on
the fame of Constable.
We are having beautiful
weather and just pottering
between one little Suffolk
village and the next.
Hope you are well
and much happier.
Don't worry about things —
life has a way of
sorting things out.

Much love."

KATHLEEN O'DONNELL

Storytime

for Sara

You tell your story everywhere. I am continually amazed
the more I hear it. Your neck has veins like a strong man's.
You turn it in conversation, smoking, arching: to see
Where your girlfriend's gone.

But where you've gone…. O you've gone all right.
Left mother Ireland, husband, children, birthplace.
Not mentioned: womenfriends, womanlovers, woman-
acquaintances. You'll not be back.

You are shorthaired and your bottom is a woman's
Round and firm. Peaches wilt at such splendour.
Though you pretend otherwise, your breasts are
Non-existent. Mother's milk had to leave
To find its true sources.

You hitch your belt up, spread your legs,
Talk of photographs of you and other women in
Miniskirts and how it looked. I don't want to talk about
How it looks.

Your face is wide, eyes small and amazed. No flinching
Through cigarette smoke. Tan imprinted into
your skin. Your web of disaster makes you more
attractive still.

You awaken suddenly, scared, when touched
In your sleep. Eyes wide and skin taut.
You don't settle easily. Only when
Outside imperative takes over.

Outside of you, of me. It's getting colder now.
I feel for your bones, those delicate traceries
of white calcium mirroring bedrooms filled with
lace.

The frost glitters. I want to warm you.
Distant whistling in the forest beckons.
Your shorn hair forms our trees. Come

JENNIFER BARRACLOUGH

The Watch Cottage

I live in different houses now.
Bigger and busier, bought to serve an end —
Nearer to work, to roads, to friends.
They're solid houses, stone-built, gardened, groomed,
Two of us knowing how to occupy each room.

This is a house I think I might have known.

I'm eight or nine. I go through fields alone.
I find the ruins of old cottages,
Grassed over, lost, a frame, a shape.
Sometimes there's wallpaper, a grate,
Cupboards with rubble, dust.

At night my father works alone
In the small house that's now a lumber store.
He takes a Tilley lamp. It hisses through the time
We're there together, while he planes
Or handles seeds and plants.

I play upstairs, in a low room
That might have sheltered three or four or more.
They're not here with me. This is no ghost-reviving exercise.
I'm by myself, with things that know their business,
Walls, floors, a certain kind of watchfulness.

It's cold. The winter's afternoon brings down the night.
Someone is coming in to speak to me, switch on the light.

KATHRYN BELL

Nothing Like This Before

The neighbours gather to pay their respects
To the son, the clever one, who went to London and died young.
Mother sits majestic, tears loom behind her bifocals.
Father pours drinks: wine for the women, whisky for the men.
Sister serves sandwiches and madeira cake.
Curiosity conquers compassion: one whispers, "What was it, then?"
Truth rises in sister like vomit; she swallows it. "A blood
    disease."
"Ah, leukaemia, likely?" "Something like that, so they said."
"It's this radiation, atomic reactors, never was nothing like it
    in my time."
All nod silently, satisfied. Never was nothing like this before.
The son too is silent, closeted in his coffin.

SHIRANI SITUNAYAKE

SOMETIMES I THINK THERE IS A CONSPIRACY

AGAINST ME
AS I STARE AT MY EFFORTS IN THE SUN,
COPPER, WALNUT, ROSEWOOD HUES,
WITH PATCHES OF RED AND WHITE,
AS IF IN SOME KIND OF DEFIANCE AND MOCKERY
MY BLACKNESS LIES SHROUDED
UNDER A WHITE PIGMENT,
REFUSING REVELATION, NURTURING OR CONTRAST.
SO I ASSUME IT MUST BE MY LOT
TO IDENTIFY THE BLACKNESS WITHIN MY SOUL:
THE DARK ROOT,
BURIED IN AMONGST THE COCONUT PALMS AND LUSH
    FRONDS:
AN ESSENCE SO VITAL STILL,
DESPITE THE YEARS OF OVERBEARING OVERLAY.
HERE MY SOUL FINDS LAUGHTER.
STILL I SEARCH
FOR PRIDE,
FOR INTEGRITY,
FOR ONENESS,
FOR WHOLENESS.
PIECING TOGETHER THE PUZZLE
OF MY SELF,
SCATTERED OVER MILES AND MILES.
AND SLOWLY I FIND THEM COMING TOGETHER
AS I LEARN TO LOVE MYSELF
A LITTLE HARDER

I USED TO SEEK THE REGULAR FAMILIAR

BREATHING OF ANOTHER FRIEND
TO KEEP MY NIGHTS LIGHTER
WHEN SLEEP ESCAPED ME.
BUT THINGS SEEM TO HAVE CHANGED:
MY BODY WILL SNUGGLE UP TO ITSELF
AND I LISTEN TO MY OWN
BREATH
FALL BETWEEN MY NOSE AND MOUTH.
SOMETIMES IN RASPS,
BUT USUALLY RELIABLE
AND ENOUGH TO KEEP ME ALIVE.
EVEN THE SHADOWS
THAT ANNOUNCED OTHER MORE FRIGHTENING SHAPES
I'VE GROWN USED TO.
THE SPACE BETWEEN THE SHEETS,
THE DENT IN THE MIDDLE OF THE MATTRESS
IS MOSTLY FILLED BY ME.
I USED TO FEEL SAD.
NOW I JUST FEEL ALONE
AND I LIKE THE CREASES
AND CRUMPLES
I
ALONE
MAKE.

ANN SLADE

.... *to* JANE

To Jane who moved in stealthily and in disguise
To Jane who dismantled the defences of a very well-defended woman
To Jane who unearthed a volcano of latent feeling
To Jane who resurrected sex and left it hanging in suspense
To Jane who for a short while succumbed
To Jane who had no experience and so was not to know
To Jane in whose name in excess of one A4 pad of paper has been
      expended in analysis of a passion, a person, of two people,
      of three people, and of their families
To Jane who is a very private person and prefers to remain a
      mystery
To Jane for whom feeling is pain
To Jane who gave not one word of encouragement to love, except in
      code
To Jane who denies
To Jane whose eyes betrayed the lies
To Jane who trusts Elizabeth
To Jane who would not take the risk
To Jane who knows both love and lust but values security more
To Jane whose stale friendship my presence revitalised
To Jane who was my Magnificent Obsession, my Fatal Attraction
To Jane who I never really knew, but knew enough for love, and
      for the insanity of love's repression
To Jane who gave, gave, gave but who could not take
To Jane who withdrew it all
To Jane who would not ask to understand
To Jane, perplexed, confused, determined
To Jane who has known cruelty and who repeated it
To Jane who felt rejected by one who felt rejected
To Jane who pretended nothing really mattered
To Jane whose reason rules her but who cannot hide her heart

JAN SELLERS

Where Lesbians Come From

It is true that lesbians do not have families;
we have pretend family relationships.
We do not have mothers, fathers, brothers, sisters;
our sons and daughters do not count at all,
having no families within which to rear them.
And our lovers, there's nothing in that
but something mocking truth.
For you know it's true —
that lesbians do not have families, like you.

We emerge, instead, complete from some dark shell,
beds and beds of us (like oysters,
what else would I mean?),
sea-born on stormy nights
with the wind in a certain quarter.
We rise and wriggle, all slippery and secret,
curling and stretching and glad to be alive,
untangling our hair from the wind and salt and seaweed.
We steal clothes from washing-lines,
and once it's daylight, almost pass for human.

Glowing into warmth in the sun or a hard north wind,
we lick the salt from our lips,
for now,
and smile.
We live for a while in the light,
(despite your wish that we were not here),
returning to our beds by moonlight
to nurture and foster the sweet salt shells
that give birth to our lesbian futures —
and there we plot, in our dark sea beds,
the seduction of your daughters.

MARGARET EASTON

On Ironing

a woman ironing hums
her family pile before her
in coloured folds of intimacy

she eats brown toffee
wrapped in opaque paper
twisted neatly at the ends

and thinks of love
of pillowcases like oblong bonbons
that smell of the garden

respectability drifts
on collars and cuffs
steam from the creases

of pockets smoothed
hisses below eye level
she tucks round

a spare pearl button
down the bright frayed inside seam
out of sight

beside her thumb
a loose white silko thread
she just might pull

Across the Sand

Would you care to take a turn,
with me   to haunt   my face
the sand   myself   to touch,
sallow reflections.

Walk the marsh on a wet afternoon.
Watch city seagulls peck
at scarlet bait in tins,
gather grass seed in the palm
of our hands.

I imagine for us
a shoreline in the early dark.

Shall we eat chocolate cake.
Will you climb my words
arms thrown out for balance,
while blue anoraks drip into the bath,
wet socks on the radiator.

Your footsteps   my forehead,
imprints across the sand.
We carry timid ghosts,
and after,
can't we pardon emptiness.

ASTRA

funeral in new york

from east twenty-eighth street
the gannon funeral home sent me a bill
for the funeral of julia shaw
once my mother

six items as follows:
thirty-five dollars for the removal from the morgue —
they call it the medical examiner's office —
ninety dollars for arrangements and supervision —
a lot of arranging and supervising
if you ask me
but then i wasn't there

there's also fifty-five dollars for the hearse
going to the crematorium in another part of town
was it pulled by a horse i wonder?
were there mourners along the way?

the casket cost a modest seventy-five dollars —
modest by american standards i guess
and the charge for the burning bit
the cremation
was the same as the supervision and arrangements —
ninety dollars

finally   six dollars and seventy-five cents
for some transcripts of death

the total   three hundred and forty-one dollars
and seventy-five cents —
all this for the barest essentials

if you call these essentials

finally the bill is paid

pussy willows

my mother has no grave for me to visit
her ashes know no
burial ground   no marker   no greenery
but the pair of pussy willow trees in my garden
stir her in my mind each january
when they bud

pussy willows were her favourite
and chinese lanterns   eucalyptus   bittersweet

yet she never saw my garden   my pussy willows   my flat
hardly knew her grandchildren/my sons
never met my friends   my cats   my poems
never witnessed me settled on my own
in my own place
with my own ways

just as well:
                she'd have been overcome with jealousy

spirit

lilacs were her favourite flower —
they're mine too

what a coincidence

next year i'll plant lilacs
in my garden
one white one purple

then i'll know she's really with me
as i know she's in the pussy willows
i've cut from my garden
and keep in a tall pottery jug
in front of my window
that looks out on to the woods

she's out there too

MAUREEN DUFFY

On the London Poetry Secretariat Poets Card

This card says I bleed
inwardly
this card says I have been treated
and there is nothing to be done for me
this card says I work
in the sewers of the human psyche
underground
that I rat
sharp toothed on what I see among my fellows
that I burrow in the sludge
to turn up dropped watches
pearls that are your eyes
it says I am high on every kind
of unnatural hallucinogen
will make cause of the commonplace
am liable to sudden collapse
in which case they must send for her
whose touch makes new and whole.
This card says there are certain things it's no good
giving me
or they poison my system
(maybe I've had enough)
like prevarication, procrastination
that make me throw up.
This card says that vital bits of me
portative organs will still be available
for service when I'm dead
such as affirmations, celebrations
voluntaries, aires to a loved ground
like this.
This card says I am a poet
I carry it with me everywhere.

Genetics

The night before he left my father cracked
the brown armour of shrimps, nipped off
the whiskery head with the black bead eyes
and the hard fantail in a labour of love
that had become a ritual of goodbye.
We never saw him again. To my two months
it hardly mattered but she must have lain alone
or pushed me as I knew from her Grimm's tales
my folklore I took her through: "Tell us
about when..." along deserted streets that led
to a shillingsworth of gas I made her
slam the oven door on with my two month wail.
My hands were like his she always said
and yet I see her hands ghost in their
gestures, plucking at my own flesh, hangnail
dry cheek, eyebrow fern as she herded crumbs
across the tablecloth with sheepdog brown fingers
or the breadknife. He could never put together
took apart with his hands that may be mine
but left the elemental cogwheels, bike chains
in primaeval chaos on the newspapered floor.
She fitted them into working order. My hands peel
a peach for you, furl back that soft skin
from the sweet globe I lust to sink
my teeth into. We both know the meaning
of peaches. Yet I can't tell whose fingers
peel so lovingly, his or hers, male or female
maker or destroyer. I splay my fingers.
The stories are thirty years dead and like all
retellers I warp, encrust, unmake.
The hands should know. Or have they learnt new gestures?
The fingers more spatulate, life and heart line
less broken than theirs? She never left
but made of the threaded chains of sputem
her lungs powered a lifeline I clung to.
Yet the eyes to see peaches, peel and present them
the hands that strip them down to naked flesh
flushed with eager juice the lips suck up
are those that ripped the scales from seafood

and gave her salt, waveborn, the small pink serpents
that caught in the sea anemone's embrace
are questing, taken in, father's fingers.

Preserves

Only the rich ate marmalade. We had red jam
that soaked through the grey bread like blood on lint.
It might have been the war we always blamed
for everything but yet inside I knew it wasn't.

Once visiting a schoolfriend, doctor's daughter
staying the night strangely in a strange house, I looked
for it at breakfast but was only offered
honey, gilt beespit to spread on leisured toast.

This Wednesday for the first time I really made it
in your country kitchen, scalded, skinned and sliced
added white drifts of sweetness to bitter fruit
and simmered til the peel was clear as the ice

we'd played with childishly that afternoon
duck and draking the jagged panes to smithereens
on the pond's skating surface, a brittle moon
you wanted to crack. The pots gleam golden

with candied slivers aswim in a sharp sauce.
Filled with you I know I'm rich too, at last.

BERTA FREISTADT

Reprimand

I do wish you two
Would stop it
Or at least restrict yourselves
To less unsocial hours.
The earth moved
Seven times last night
Between nine-thirty
And five
And I have to be up for work.
Also the world
Is in enough chaos
Without you adding to it.
You must not suck
Rivers dry
Nor scream down avalanches
There are others to think of.
Wendy and Moira
of Gisburn, Lancs
Paddling at Whitstable
On their first holiday
For years
Will not thank you
If they must chase the waves
For ten miles
Under a scarlet sky
Because you two
Made the moon blush
And miss her turn.

As for me,
When at two forty-five
Portknockie flipped
And felt the spray
As the ferry docked
At Shanklin I.O.W.
And fishermen shook
And blamed the small catch

On those sounds
Welling from the deep
Frightening the fish,
My "Politics of Celibacy"
Fell off the shelf
And hit me on the nose.
Before I could
Laugh at the irony
You did it again
And I nearly fell out of bed.

What a night!

SHIRLEY PICTON

we can't think
every issue
through
to its logical conclusion
confusion
tonight
when we are struggling to survive

we cannot fight every battle today
or watch every word we say

our pain and loss are equal
not more or less
we may not be bottom of any heap
but the mountain we climb each day
exhausts us   just the same
our children are neglected
we have nothing left to give them

our tide recedes
leaving a few words
on a deserted beach
if "In the recognition of loving lies an answer to despair"*

then   yes we love
but we also despair
of not having the strength
equal to the task
of loving
equally.

*Audre Lorde

memories

is it you that haunts me
i can see you clearer now
with long grey hair
twisted round and round into a bun
fixed with pins
in your dark red crepe dress
and the sweet smell of cologne
you rubbed across my head
the one who loved as it ought to be

why did you not teach me to play the piano
or to sing
i remember none of these things about you
only your pink corset
that i helped to hook
and the feather bed
and the crack in the bathroom sink
and the cat had kittens
you were afraid of treading on them
you went to whist drives
believed in god
sang in the choir   mother said
your roots were welsh
do i hear you sing now

side by side we walked
alike   people said
you bought me barley sugar sticks
and gave me threepenny bits
i ran from home to you
with a suitcase of teddies and dolls
but they stopped me

then you had a stroke in my bed
my room
they sent me to a birthday party
on the day of your funeral
so i sat in a corner and cried
and i cry again when i remember you
is that the way it ought to be

GER KILLEEN

To Her Lover

Be coy
My sweet defenceless
Little foe,
And I will take you to me
For a friend.
Be gentle, subtle,
Be less of
Your own,
And I will
Alter anger, and unbend
My joy,
The fractured wish
To mend.

And long, sad songs,
Let siren-hearts defend!

LOUISE CAROLIN

here we are again

here we are again
the places same as usual
disagreement corrupting
our shared air
we blame eachother
for our common
inability to see the
other's point of view.
i'll run myself a bath-
full of hot water
deep clear lapping
and lower myself in
to its depths feel it
licking my edges.
you've gone out i heard
the door slam
but i know you
i know you'll soon be back
and i'll be waiting
clean forgiving
for your cold fingers
at my temples
your lips warming
at my neck.

in a world where words

look now you was
one expensive woman
in a world where words
are all i got to give
i played profligate
i guess it serve me right
i spent words all my
words all i got to give
and you just swallow
em up with your silence so
i'm empty sick and tired
i learn at least what's precious
save it up and distribute wisely
else all you left with is
something ragged inside

MAGGIE CHRISTIE

Listening to the radio 2nd of february 1988

In the morning, a Bach cantata:
Leichtgesinnte Flattergeister.
An aria on flibbertigibbets — frivolous souls.
An arioso on sin.
More about sin.
More about souls.
But finally, something about trumpets and D major.

In the evening, the hya hya show:
The Lords debate Clause 28.
An aria on our right to exist.
An arioso on sin.
More about sin.
More about rights.
Sin wins —
They vote: we may have no rights.
We are badly in need of trumpets and D major.

cottaging

gratification
with a stiff upper lip
would be hard to imagine
if it weren't for the fact that
i play the oboe

MARY JO BANG

In a Book of Original Entry

I

I'm sure you thought I would forget.
How long, after all,
does a child's mind
hold a thing?
Seven and delirious
with scarlet fever;
did I really crawl that night,
as I remember?
I know it took forever
to pick my way through
that dark walled space
which hung between our rooms,
a curtain of uncertainty,
and fear.
And standing, finally,
at my mother's side,
I whispered:
mother.

It was, instead,
your rasping voice which returned:
GET BACK TO BED.
DON'T BOTHER YOUR MOTHER.
I must have spoken,
or started to,
when your ever ready anger
came hissing towards me
like hot steam:
YOU HEARD ME.
IF I GET OUT OF THIS BED, YOU'LL BE SORRY.

Time melted afterwards.
In a room as dark as a dream,
I heard words and wondered what they meant.
No one was allowed to enter,
but sometimes I would wake

from my seamless sleep
to find my sister
watching from the doorway
and my mother on the
narrow edge of my bed,
humming a soft song —
a melody which always rests
just out of reach.

II

You look pale against
white hospital sheets,
the cut in your throat
a brightly coloured wound
which must never heal.
Your cancerous vocal cords
now preserved for ever
in formaldehyde.

I sit very still on the edge of your bed,
careful not to wake you,
except for a moment of impersonal pity
when I wipe the saliva from your chin.
You move and I wish you back to sleep,
hoping to avoid that unwelcome sight
of your swollen mouth forming
itself around soundless words.
I am weary already of trying to understand you.
Your unsteady hand writes me messages
Pain when I swallow.
What time?
I wonder what memories lie
behind your closed eyes,
what dreams ripple your thin lids.
Do you ever search for words?
Something which will tie
the unutterable past into today?
Or am I the only one,
daughter of silence,
who refuses to forget;
writing everything down,
recording each receipt
in a book of original entry.

I Am Writing

(for R.W.)

Dear Doctor,
I am writing to request the return
of my words.
I suspect there are thousands by now,
if not millions.
I assume you still have these,
perhaps in a shoebox
hidden under the floorboards.

I would have sworn that someone was
even taking photographs:
me as a madwoman,
me as a snarling dog,
me as a good girl with you as the father,
the day we went to Disneyland.
There must be enough for an album.

Surely there is some chronicle of the weeping.
Not simply a list of the tears and their sources
but one which describes each slight
in great detail
and stars every near fatal wound.

I find it hard to believe that
no one was keeping a record —
at least of the pills.
The yellows which changed nothing;
the greens which turned life into dreamland;
all day I chased boogeymen
down dark alleyways.

Someone should have been writing this down.
You, especially, must know
that memory can never be trusted.

Open Heart Surgery

The initial incision
begins as a fine line,
which widens until it forms a river
wet with red rain
drawn from its own banks.
As one penetrates deeper and deeper,
the bleeding becomes more and more
difficult to control
and every new layer is another
piece of armor which must be pierced.
At last, the sternum is separated
and the prize is brought forward,
still beating, and placed on the chest.
The miracle is that a heart
can be so impassionately handled
and still survive.
It's a lot like love, actually.
And in both cases, there comes a point
when it is not unwise
to pause and say a silent prayer
for that pale body beneath,
which so patiently waits
to experience great pain.

GILLIAN HANSCOMBE

From "Some of Sybil"

In the guise

In the guise of Artemis, hunter, you can ride me all the way to the sun; and be ridden back again. Your bow-arm is stronger than an olive-stump, though your hands are smooth as plums. When you pour libations, my ears sting with the brim and swish of your words. I adore the bowstring pulled taut; the symptoms of desire.

Does she know

Does she know
           when she's standing, speaking
         (gowned and silky)
so unlikely maybe or
untimely in this public circumstance
          that (how) I romance?
I admit I mean to undo,
unfasten, in my own presence also standing, smiling,
for my own enhancing.
         (Naked most fluent, better than
any divine drapery; and excellently skilled.)
As fictive as a hologram, you might reply.
But I, who have held all manner of flesh and grass,
         defiant ferns, fish even,
           and the whack of unkind water,
willingly commit idolatry.
       Does she know
when she's standing, speaking,
with what unlikely images
         I must contend?

ASPEN

loving song

stretch marks
silver lines
pattern of twigs
and shadows
on your breasts
smell of
the forest
wet dew
soft and tough
grass
beech buds
open out softly
into leaves
around
my lips.

KATE HALL

Eye Catching

Caught your eye
Again
well it can't just
be me
can it?
I mean
you must
look at me
even if
it's only
to see
if I'm
looking
at you
which of course
sometimes
I am
even
if it's only
to see…

we stay
eyes locked
for hour long
seconds
my mind
goes blank
what I feel
has no words
or pictures
for describing…

I want you

I struggle
hoping
my wanting

isn't
over flowing
spilling out
in public
hoping
you
see nothing.

One of us
sometimes
you
this time
me
looks away
not just
with our
eyes
no
the whole
head
turns
stating clearly
I
wasn't
looking
anyway.

GILLIAN SPRAGGS

Riddle Game

for Mog

It is a tower on a wooded hill.
Below, a secret well seeps elixir.
Unicorns drink there.

It is the crest on a strange creature.
Watch as it rears and stiffens.
The mouth opens slowly, like a rose.

It is a dolphin in a troubled sea,
leaping and turning.
The waves are full of weed; they taste of salt.

It is the mouthpiece of a deep recorder
mellow in tone, and vibrant.
Touch the hole with your finger: hear the note vary.

It is a ridge of folded rock
over a cave with glistening walls.
There are earthquakes in that country.

KYDE WILLOWMOON

One Minute

In one minute
i could
kiss you — fast —
a dozen times,

or
one, long,
slow and trippy,
honey-drippy.

i could
speak of love
in seven tongues,
in Celtic fires
and Mediterranean suns,

or
Spell your name
in
Irish lines,
entwine
with mine,

or
braid your hair
with fireweed,
find opal seed
love need

and
laughing,
slip some softly spice.

i could
live three life-times long
and weave wild wings of siren song,
yet cannot stay the passing,
one minute here,
one minute
gone.

BIOGRAPHICAL NOTES

ASTRA was born in Manhattan in 1927 and has lived in London since 1962. She is the author of three published collections of poetry: *fighting words, battle cries* and *Back You Come, Mother Dear* (Virago, 1986). Her work has appeared in many anthologies. She is the mother of two sons.

MARY JO BANG was born in 1946 in Waynesville, Missouri, escaped to St Louis when she was six moths old. Later, she received a B.A. and M.A. in Sociology from Northwestern University, Evanston, Illinois. She moved to London in 1986 and completed a B.A. in Photography at the Polytechnic of Central London. Her poems have been published in many magazines in the U.K. and the U.S.

JENNIFER BARRACLOUGH Born 1945 in Cardiff of Yorkshire-Welsh parentage, has lived mostly in Yorkshire, the last decade fortunately with someone of rather broader horizons. Is a Quaker, has been a teacher, a pub landlady and latterly an arts administrator. Recently completed an M.A. in Cultural Studies, with a dissertation on feminists and crime fiction. Writes extremely infrequently.

KATHRYN BELL was born in 1934 in Glasgow. She began writing poems and short stories in 1977 upon joining the Gay Authors Workshop. She is a member of Gemma and Gay Vegetarians. Her work has appeared in the Oscars Press pamphlets *Teatime at Sarah's* and *Sugar & Snails*.

ANNIE BLUE: working class lesbian feminist. Born in a Lancashire mill town. Eventually escaped catholicism but not a convent school education. Lurched into college in Liverpool via graphic design and banking. Taught. Became a lesbian/feminist/angry. Dropped out and into working towards women's liberation in groups like Women Against Violence Against Women. Started to take myself seriously — write poetry and read it, make art and show it. Now live in Hackney. Work as head of Art at an East London girls school, bringing up my daughter Amy aged 4, and on the collective of the Revolutionary & Radical Feminist Magazine. Want to live off my art work and writing, learn to weave, play the saxophone, have more time to do what I want, be part of a women's revolution.

JEANNIE BREHAUT is Canadian, 26 years old, has lived in London for 7 years. She works as a full-time waitress and writes prose as well as poetry. Her short stories have appeared in magazines and her essays were included in *Delighting the Heart* (Women's Press, 1989).

LOUISE CAROLIN was born in 1966 and grew up in S.E. London. She came out at age 19 with relief. Since then, she has spent three years studying in Cambridge and working with *Shocking Pink*. She writes that she is now living in New Cross and resisting the temptation to have a kitten. She dedicates her poems to her bicycle, Edge, stolen, 25/9/89.

MAGGIE CHRISTIE was born in 1952 and grew up in the south of England. After getting through being a born-again Christian, she became a political activist, a mother, a born-again feminist and a born-again lesbian in quick succession. She then moved to Edinburgh, where she has lived ever since. She recently became a born-again oboist. She is a member of two writing groups, one "womens", one "dykes", without which she would have a lot more difficulty allowing herself to finish poems in between her work deadlines as an indexer and editor. She also helps to produce Edinburgh Women's Liberation Newsletter, writes and plays music, researches women composers. She recently won a prize for performance poetry and has a poem in the Stramullion anthology *Fresh Oceans*.

ELEANOR DARE was born in 1965 near the river Thames in London. Later she went to art school where she felt isolated. "I was the only Lesbian I knew. Now I live with Amanda and Miss Trowbridge. We are all Lesbians."

MANDY DEE died on 30 October 1988, at the age of 35 years. Caroline Halliday is her Literary Executrix. The poem "Night" which appears in this volume, was previously published by *Sinister Wisdom* (USA); her work also appears in *The Carmen Thread* and *Serious Pleasure*. Before her death, she wrote of herself: "I am white, born working class, lesbian feminist, with anarchist tendencies, bedbound with Multiple Sclerosis. I was born spastic, brought up as a disabled child, so in my mid-twenties I began to be an adult disabled from birth who also had progressive disease. There are not many women in England with that experience. When I write anything, it is a race between ability and exhaustion to get it down before I become too physically tired to think or write. I live in south London and have fought rivers of blood to get the house I now have. The situation for disabled housing is desperate."

MAUREEN DUFFY was born in 1933 in Worthing, Sussex, and educated in state schools and at King's College, London. She became a full-time writer in 1962 after the success of her first novel, *That's How It Was*, which has recently been republished by Virago. Since then, she has published twelve novels and had six plays performed, as well as writing non-fiction. Her *Collected Poems: 1949-1984* was published by Hamish Hamilton in 1985.

MARGARET EASTON lives in London where she belongs to a women's writing workshop. Her writing has been published in magazines.

U.A. FANTHORPE was born in Kent in 1929 and educated at Oxford. She has authored four volumes of poetry published by Peterloo: *Side Effects* (1978), *Standing To* (1982), *Voices Off* (1984), and *A Watching Brief* (1987). Her *Selected Poems* was published by Penguin Books in 1986. She has been the recipient of numerous prizes and fellowships. She lives in Gloucestershire.

BERTA FREISTADT is a Londoner. Her writing appears in both Britain and the U.S., in several anthologies of short stories, poetry and plays. She has been a writer since the age of six but wonders if it was ever a good idea, perhaps she could have been rich instead.

CAROLINE GRIFFIN was born in 1950 in the Midlands. She teaches in a boy's comprehensive school in London and lives in a women's house. She is the co-parent of a daughter, aged 10. She is the author of a collection of poems, *Passion is Everywhere Appropriate* (Onlywomen, 1989). Her poems have appeared in *One Foot on the Mountain* and *Beautiful Barbarians* (Onlywomen) and *Naming the Waves* (Virago). She co-authors plays with Maro Green — *Mortal* was performed at the Women's Theatre Group at the Young Vic Studio in London and on national tour.

KATE HALL was born in 1945 and describes herself as a white, working class, lesbian mother and grandmother who lives in Hammersmith with a dog and three cats. Her work has appeared in *Naming the Waves* (Virago) and other anthologies. She works as a movement/dance tutor and assertiveness trainer with adults with learning disabilities. She is currently working on a novel.

CAROLINE HALLIDAY is the author of a collection of poems, *Some Truth, Some Change*. Her work appears in *Naming the Waves* (Virago) and *One Foot on the Mountain* (Onlywomen). She is a co-mother and is currently co-editing an anthology of creative writing for lesbians on issues around children. She combines writing with working as an independent consultant, and teaching a lesbian creative writing class in London.

GILLIAN HANSCOMBE was born in Melbourne, Australia, in 1945. She has lived in England since 1955. Her books include *Hecate's charms, Rocking the Cradle* (with Jackie Forster), *The Art of Life, Title Fight* (with Andrew Lumsden) and *Flesh and Paper* (with Suniti Namjoshi; Jezebel, 1986). Her work appears in *Naming the Waves* (Virago) and *Beautiful Barbarians* (Onlywomen). She has one son.

GER KILLEEN is Irish and lives in London.

DOROTHY NIMMO was born in 1932 in Manchester, educated in York and Cambridge. She has published two books of poetry, *A Woman's Work* (Brazen Voices, 1984), and *Homewards* (Giant Steps, 1987). Her short stories have been included in Faber's *First Fictions* and *Introduction 9*, and her poems have appeared in countless magazines. She has been, from time to time, actress, mother of four, gardener and goatherd.

KATHLEEN O'DONNELL is 27 years old and studies European history at the University of Ulster at Coleraine. She is interested in women, children, astrology and Jewish history.

SHIRLEY PICTON is 36 years old and a 3rd year B.A. student of English and Theatre Arts. She has had some articles and stories published. "I became more interested in poetry in the last two or three years after the break-up of a 15 year marriage and realization of my lesbianism. I have two children who do not at present live with my lover and me."

SUZANNA RASMUSSEN was born in Denmark in 1950, has taught in London for some years, has performed in poetry/song cabaret with a trio called BRIX, and solo as Eva Brick. She has a collection of poetry entitled *Punch the Ceiling* on tape with Feminist Audio Books. Her unfulfilled ambitions are: to win the Wimbledon Tennis Tournament, and to become a freelance superwoman.

JAN SELLERS is 38 years old and lives in Leyton with her cat, Michita. She organises adult and community education classes and occasionally teaches. Her poems have appeared in several magazines: *Tears in the Fence* (Dorset), *Common Lives, Lesbian Lives* (USA), *Rites* (Canada) and will appear in a forthcoming poetry anthology published by Community Projects Foundation, London.

SHIRANI SITUNAYAKE "I am 32 years old. Born in Sri Lanka. Came to England when I was 7 years old. Self employed carpenter. Recovering alcohol and drug abuser. Have been "out" since I was 14, but have always been a lesbian. My life has been eclipsed for many years by self abuse and prison but now in my third year of sobriety, I am embracing life, old and treasured friendships, and a new found joy in being a black lesbian."

ANN SLADE "I'm in mid-life and quite old enough to know better than to get carried away by the greatest passion of my life. I was teaching, but am no longer ... I could provide you with a heartfelt understanding of the menopause, by the way."

GILLIAN SPRAGGS was born in 1952 and educated at Girton College, Cambridge. "Over many years of mostly not writing poems, I have gradually learned to ignore my two internal censors: the self-oppressed, self-silencing lesbian, and even more deadly, academic literary critic." She has published a number of reviews, articles and essays, many about lesbian and gay issues in education, and edited and contributed to *Outlaws in the Classroom: Lesbians and Gays in the School System*. Her study of Sylvia Townsend Warner and Valentine Ackland is included in the forthcoming collection *Lesbian and Gay Writing* (Macmillan).

SARAH WALKER is teaching in Naples.

KYDE WILLOWMOON lives in the Yorkshire Dales with her 10 year old daughter. She makes cards and mobiles, studies aromatherapy and massage, writes, sings, eats smoked tofu and laughs quite a lot.